ideals®
EASTER

More Than 50 Years of Celebrating Life's Most Treasured Moments
Vol. 55, No. 1

"Again the ancient miracle, as new

As though it had not been!

Blossom by blossom, bell by bell,

The south wind ushers Easter in."

—*Nancy Byrd Turner*

America the Beautiful 6	From the Bible 36	Our Heritage 70
From My Garden Journal 10	Through My Window 48	Legendary Americans 72
Country Chronicle 16	Handmade Heirloom 56	Remember When 76
Readers' Reflections 20	Ideals' Family Recipes 58	For the Children 78
A Slice of Life 26	Collector's Corner 64	Bits & Pieces 82
Devotions from the Heart 32	Traveler's Diary 68	Readers' Forum 86

IDEALS—Vol. 55, No. 1 January MCMXCVIII IDEALS (ISSN 0019-137X) is published six times a year: January, March, May, July, September, and November by IDEALS PUBLICATIONS INCORPORATED, 535 Metroplex Drive, Suite 250, Nashville, TN 37211.
Periodical postage paid at Nashville, Tennessee, and additional mailing offices.
Copyright © MCMXCVIII by IDEALS PUBLICATIONS INCORPORATED.
POSTMASTER: Send address changes to Ideals, PO Box 305300, Nashville, TN 37230. All rights reserved.
Title IDEALS registered U.S. Patent Office.

SINGLE ISSUE—U.S. $5.95 USD; Higher in Canada
ONE-YEAR SUBSCRIPTION—U.S. $19.95 USD; Canada $36.00 CDN (incl. GST and shipping); Foreign $25.95 USD
TWO-YEAR SUBSCRIPTION—U.S. $35.95 USD; Canada $66.50 CDN (incl. GST and shipping); Foreign $47.95 USD

The paper used in this publication meets the minimum requirements of
American National Standard for Information Sciences—
Permanence of Paper for Printed Library Materials, ANSI Z39.48-1984.

Subscribers may call customer service at 1-800-558-4343 to make address changes.
Unsolicited manuscripts will not be returned without a self-addressed, stamped envelope.

ISBN 0-8249-1147-4   GST 131903775

Cover Photo
PINK TULIPS AND BLUE IRISES
D. Petku/H. Armstrong Roberts

Inside Front Cover
CHILDREN IN A POPPY FIELD
Dianne E. Flynn, artist
Christie's Images

Inside Back Cover
THE WATER MEADOW
Dianne E. Flynn, artist
Christie's Images

TO MY SISTER

It is the first mild day of March:
　Each minute sweeter than before,
The redbreast sings from the tall larch
　That stands beside our door.

There is a blessing in the air,
　Which seems a sense of joy to yield
To the bare trees, and mountains bare,
　And grass in the green field.

My Sister! ('tis a wish of mine)
　Now that our morning meal is done,
Make haste, your morning task resign;
　Come forth and feel the sun.

Edward will come with you—and, pray,
　Put on with speed your woodland dress,
And bring no book; for this one day
　We'll give to idleness.

No joyless forms shall regulate
　Our living calendar;
We from today, my Friend, will date
　The opening of the year.

Love, now a universal birth,
　From heart to heart is stealing;
From earth to man, from man to earth:
　—It is the hour of feeling.

One moment now may give us more
　Than years of toiling reason;
Our minds shall drink at every pore
　The spirit of the season.

Some silent laws our hearts will make,
　Which they shall long obey;
We for the year to come may take
　Our temper from today.

And from the blessed power that rolls
　And, below, above,
We'll frame the measure of our souls:
　They shall be tuned to love.

Then come, my Sister! Come, I pray,
　With speed put on your woodland dress;
And bring no book: for this one day
　We'll give to idleness.

William Wordsworth

Daffodils bloom beneath the shelter of an ancient oak tree when spring arrives in Callaway Gardens, Pine Mountain, Georgia.
Photograph by William Johnson/Johnson's Photography.

These beautiful days most enrich all my life.

—John Muir

Invocation of the Dawn

Look to this day!
For it is life, the very life of life.
In its brief course lies all the verities,
All the realities of existence:
The bliss of growth,
The glory of action,
The splendor of beauty:

For yesterday is always a dream,
And tomorrow is only a vision;
But today, well-lived,
Makes every yesterday a dream of happiness,
And every tomorrow a dream of hope.
Look well, therefore, to this day.

Kalidasa

So here hath been dawning
Another blue day;
Think, wilt thou let it
Slip useless away?

Thomas Carlyle

At Break of Day

I like to rise up early
Just before the break of day
When all is still and quiet
And the world seems miles away.

In through an open window drifts
Sweet scent of dew-drenched air;
Like lilies on an altar,
It calls my heart to prayer.

It's here within this quiet time
All stress and worries cease.
I seek God's guidance for my day
And find an inner peace.

The sun breaks through above the hill
To herald a new day
While the rose-pink mist of early dawn
Slowly fades away.

I love the early morning hour,
The day as yet untrod,
When all the world is quiet and still
And I'm alone with God.

Kay Hoffman

Day breaks in glorious color on Oregon's Powder River. Photograph by Dennis Frates/Oregon Scenics.

Whether strolling along the flower-scented paths or quietly listening for the carols of songbirds, visitors to the Shore Acres

State Park near Coos Bay, Oregon, welcome the season of rebirth. Photograph by Dennis Frates/Oregon Scenics.

ANNUAL MIRACLE

The annual miracle approaches. Rows
Of sharp green bayonets appear to charge
The sudden snow and wind. The jonquils march
In orderly battalions, valiantly
Obedient to the call of Spring. From trees
Whose bleak and lifeless branches claw the air

"Ancilla" tulips intermingle with White Muscari grape hyacinths in Missouri. Photograph by Gay Bumgarner.

Will soon unfold the tender, shiny green
Of silken leaves. What human power
Could force the fragile texture through the hard
Coarse bark, or place the pulsing growth within
The dormant wood? The annual miracle
Approaches. Once again life is revealed
A thing immortal, contradicting all
We seem to see, and one remembers, "Why
Should it be thought a thing incredible . . .
That God should raise the dead?" Each Easter morn
The lilies bring this message to mankind.
Each year the miracle unfolds before
Our blind, unseeing eyes. Each year the Spring
Again proclaims life's immortality
And writes with Nature's pen, "The Christ is risen!"

Isla Paschal Richardson

From My Garden Journal
by Deana Deck

HYACINTH

Spring never comes early enough to suit me. I could solve the problem by moving farther south, but I am also a four-season person. I like long, hot summers; warm, brilliant autumns; cold, snowy winters; and glorious, balmy springs. I want it all. The problem is, once the holidays are over and the scents of pine and holly and apples and cinnamon no longer permeate the air, time seems to slow down. The cold, gray days plod at a snail's pace toward Easter and the return of spring.

At least they used to, before I found the cure: hyacinths. Although lilies are traditionally associated with the Easter observance, the hyacinth (*Hyacinthus*) gets my vote as the perfect plant for celebrating the return of spring.

For one thing, the colors of the hyacinth—deep blues and pinks—echo the rich pastels of Easter eggs, which makes them ideal for decorating a table for Easter brunch. Or, if a centerpiece of Easter eggs is your focal point, set them off with contrasting white hyacinths.

The fragrance of the hyacinth can

only be described as magical. I once had a windowless office in a wall-to-wall gray building. The walls were gray, the carpet was gray, and the furniture was gray. To keep from going totally mad, I kept fresh flowers on my desk and, in the dead of winter, replaced the bouquets with massed containers of forced hyacinth bulbs. Their seductive fragrance wafted out of my office, down the hallways and stairwells, and drew coworkers by the dozens to my door.

Although hyacinths are a mainstay of my spring garden, one reason I like them is the utter simplicity of forcing them to bloom whenever you like. All you need to do is pick a date: Easter Sunday, a birthday, an anniversary.

I aim my first batch of the season for the middle of January; so after the Christmas tree is history and the holiday poinsettias and amaryllis have given up the ghost, there is something equally colorful and fragrant to fill the void. I start a few more hyacinths every couple of weeks.

Once you decide when you want fresh hyacinth blooms, simply count back six to eight weeks. Since the bulb needs to form a good root system, a specific blooming date is hard to predict, but you can cheat a little by planting a succession of bulbs a week or so apart. That way you can be assured of having them in bloom for celebrating Easter or any other occasion. Once they bloom, the hyacinth blossoms will last about two weeks.

If you purchase your bulbs early, keep them in the refrigerator until it's time to force them. This lets you take advantage of the large assortment available in fall and keeps the bulbs from sprouting too early.

Once your start date arrives, collect your

containers and fill them with water or a combination of pebbles and water. Some stores carry hyacinth vases with a tapered top that will hold the bulb out of the water while allowing the roots full access to the water, but shallow bowls filled with gravel, glass bottles with wide mouths, or even ice cream sundae dishes will suffice.

Set each bulb on a layer of pebbles or insert three toothpicks gently into the outer surface of the bulb and balance the bulb over the water-filled container. Be careful not to let the bulb rest in the water, which could cause it to rot. It should be placed just above the surface. If you use pebbles, set the bulb on the pebbles, fill the container to just below the bulb, then add more pebbles to create a support for the bulb.

Put the containers in a dark, cool place (50° to 60° F) until they form a good root mass. Usually this will take two to four weeks. Monitor the water level during this time to be sure the newly formed roots do not dry out. A small piece of charcoal added to the water will keep it fresh.

When the bulbs have produced sprouts about two inches to three inches high, move them into a cool location with indirect light; a north window is ideal. After several days you can place them in full, indirect sunlight. Once the blooms appear, you can make them last longer by keeping them away from heat and direct light.

Although many sources advise discarding the bulbs after blooming has ceased, I've found that hyacinths which have been forced, unlike many other bulb plants, will often survive to bloom the following year when transplanted into the garden in spring, especially if the foliage has not died back. Plant them five or six inches deep and amend the soil generously with bulb food.

Of course, it's not necessary to force hyacinths for spring bloom. When planted in a sunny garden in fall they will bloom as early as April in temperate climates, later in colder areas. If you want to enjoy their heady fragrance indoors, however, forcing is the best choice since the flowers' short stems and large, barrel-shaped blossom clusters make them difficult to arrange as cut flowers.

Another type of hyacinth also serves as an early harbinger of spring and is delightful when forced or grown in the garden and cut to be displayed in miniature containers. These are the grape hyacinths (*Muscari sp.*). Grape hyacinths are small plants, reaching only six or seven inches high. They will grow in full sun or partial shade, making them ideal for rock gardens, shade gardens, and as companion plants for early tulips, bleeding hearts, or daffodils.

Grape hyacinths can also be forced. It will take about twelve weeks, so plant in November for March or April flowers, earlier for midwinter blooms. Cluster as many of the small bulbs as possible in a single pot for the best display, with the tops of the bulbs planted even with the rim of the pot. Use a soil mix consisting of two parts rich garden soil and one part peat moss or sand. Water the pot well and place in a darkened, cool, frost-free location. Ideal temperatures range from 35° to 45° F, so an unheated attic, attached garage, or even a spare refrigerator will do. Check the soil periodically and keep it barely damp. When sprouts are about two inches long, gradually move the container into a warmer, brighter location, but avoid direct sun.

One of the ways I like to bring the colors of spring into my home as early as possible is to display bouquets of cut grape hyacinth blooms in miniature containers at each place setting for brunch or dinner on Easter Sunday. A larger container of forced hyacinth blooms set into an Easter basket and surrounded with colorful jelly-beans makes a delightful centerpiece that is filled with the fragrance and color of spring.

Deana Deck tends to her flowers, plants, and vegetables at her home in Nashville, Tennessee, where her popular garden column is a regular feature in The Tennessean.

SPRING POOLS

These pools that, though in forests, still reflect
The total sky almost without defect,
And like the flowers beside them, chill and shiver,
Will like the flowers beside them soon be gone,
And yet not out by any brook or river,
But up by roots to bring dark foliage on.

The trees that have it in their pent-up buds
To darken nature and be summer woods—
Let them think twice before they use their powers
To blot out and drink up and sweep away
These flowery waters and these watery flowers
From snow that melted only yesterday.

Robert Frost

SPRINGTIME

How faithfully the lake reflects
The beauty of a peaceful scene,
Where spring, arrayed in new attire,
Has donned a gay chapeau of green.
Sharp etched against an azure sky,
Tall pine trees whisper words of cheer,
And birdsongs from the meadows rise
To spread the news that spring is here.

Brian F. King

Spring Quiet

Gone were but the Winter,
    Come were but the Spring,
I would go to a covert
    Where the birds sing;

Where in the whitethorn
    Singeth a thrush,
And a robin sings
    In the holly-bush.

Full of fresh scents
    Are the budding boughs
Arching high over
    A cool green house;

Full of sweet scents,
    And whispering air
Which sayeth softly:
    "We spread no snare;

"Here dwell in safety,
    Here dwell alone,
With a clear stream
    And a mossy stone.

"Here the sun shineth
    Most shadily;
Here is heard an echo
    Of the far sea,
Though far off it be."

Christina Rossetti

For Joy

For each and every joyful thing,
For twilight swallows on the wing,
For all that nests and all that sings—

For fountains cool that laugh and leap,
For rivers running to the deep,
For happy, care-forgetting sleep—

For stars that pierce the somber dark,
For morn, awaking with the lark,
For life new-stirring 'neath the bark—

For sunshine and the blessed rain,
For budding grove and blossoming lane,
For the sweet silence of the plain—

For bounty springing from the sod,
For every step by beauty trod—
For each dear gift of joy, thank God!

Florence Earle Coates

The true way to live is to
enjoy every moment as it passes,
and surely it is in the everyday
things around us that the beauty
of life lies.

Laura Ingalls Wilder

Springtime represents new birth in the form of two fuzzy ducklings. Photograph by Superstock.
A young girl gathers wildflowers in a sheep meadow. Photograph by Andreas/Zefa/H. Armstrong Roberts.
A wild rose peeks through the mountain dogwood in Kootenay National Park, Canada. Photograph by Dennis Frates/Oregon Scenics.

Country
CHRONICLE
Lansing Christman

Meditations by a Mountain Stream

This is Easter. Let us pause for a while by a mountain stream to muse and meditate. Here we can pray, praising the splendor of God's creation in this season of renewal, this new beginning.

How loftily the mountain on the opposite side of the stream lifts its giant shoulders toward the sun of the soft spring skies! It brings to mind Thoreau's timeless words, "Mountains are the stepping stones to heaven."

Looking up toward the peak high above does seem appropriate for this holy hour. There is the pinnacle, the apex, pointing like a steeple or a spire on a church toward the kingdom of glory. We are awed by the beauty and magnificence. We are given assurance of eternal life.

What do we hear in the singing waters plunging down over the waterfalls? And what do we hear as the waters bubble ever so gently downstream over the rocks and boulders? They are not surging and gushing anymore. They are easing along, sounding their murmuring chords. The purling melodies come from the fingers of tranquil waters pressing against the keys of rock and stone like a musician pressing the polished keys of a piano or an organ. These are gentle and restful tones.

How richly the water's music comforts us and puts our minds at ease. The tinkling sounds are consoling, as comforting as the hymns we sing and hear in the churches across the land.

Listening to the music, we realize these very chords will in time meet the massive waters of the ocean, joining the cresting waves and tides, adding glory to the endless symphony of the sea, adding glory to life. And we give thanks for the glory of God's world at Eastertime.

The author of two published books, Lansing Christman has been contributing to Ideals *for more than twenty years. Mr. Christman has also been published in several American, foreign, and braille anthologies. He lives in rural South Carolina.*

A trickling stream wends through the wildflowers in Bird Creek Meadows, Washington. Photograph by Dennis Frates/Oregon Scenics.

The Lily of the Resurrection

While the lily dwells in the earth,
Walled about with crumbling mold,
She the secret of her birth
Guesses not, nor has been told.

Hides the brown bulb in the ground,
Knowing not she is a flower;
Knowing not she shall be crowned
As a queen, with white-robed power.

Though her whole life is one thrill
Upward, unto skies unseen,
In her husks she wraps her still,
Wondering what her visions mean.

Shivering, while the bursting scales
Leave her heart bare, with a sigh
She her unclad state bewails,
Whispering to herself, "I die."

Die? Then may she welcome death,
Leaving darkness underground,
Breathing out her sweet, free breath
Into the new heavens around.

Die? She bathes in ether warm:
Beautiful without, within,
See at last the imprisoned form
All its fair proportions win!

Life it means, this impulse high
Which through every rootlet stirs:
Lo! the sunshine and the sky
She was made for, now are hers!

Soul, thou too art set in earth,
Heavenward through the dark to grow:
Dreamest thou of thy royal birth?
Climb! and thou shalt surely know.

Shuddering Doubt to Nature cries—
Nature, though she smiles, is dumb—
"How then can the dead arise?
With what body do they come?"

Lo, the unfolding mystery!
We shall bloom, some wondrous hour,
As the lily blooms, when she
Dies a bulb, to live a flower!

Lucy Larcom

Easter lilies and purple iris set the tone for a meditative Easter morning. Photograph by Al Riccio.

Readers' Reflections

Editor's Note: Readers are invited to submit unpublished, original poetry for possible publication in future issues of Ideals. *Please send typed copies only; manuscripts will not be returned. Writers receive $10 for each published submission. Send material to Readers' Reflections, Ideals Publications Inc., P.O. Box 305300, Nashville, Tennessee 37230-5300.*

IT'S SPRING

The meadows now are lush and green
   With buttercups along the stream.
Pink apple blossoms crown the trees,
   A rendezvous for honey bees.

Young robins peer from out of nest,
   Anticipating wings to test.

Purple iris edge the creeks
   Where ducklings quack with yellow beaks.

There are fluffy chicks with mother hen;
   From hidden nests parade her ten.
And near the orchard bluebirds sing—
   They too are happy that it's spring!

Mary Masten Kimmel
Surprise, Arizona

HANDS

The hands of a farmer
   Are stained from the soil.
The hands of a blacksmith
   Are calloused from toil.

Hands tell a story
   Of every man's life;

They may tell of riches
   Or hard work and strife.

But the hands of the Carpenter
   Scarred by a nail
Are the hands we must cling to,
   For they never fail.

Betty Lewallen
Heber Springs, Arkansas

GOD'S BEAUTY

The sun streams in my window;
    The dew sits on the sill.
The beauty of the morning
    Is in the robin's trill.
The lilacs are all blooming;
    The roses smell so sweet.
I wake up mid this wondrous scene,
    A new day to greet.
A little touch of heaven
    Abides outside these walls,
And in its vibrant glory
    To me it seems to call.
I'll live within God's beauty
    Until He does return
And takes me home on high,
    Of greater things to learn.
So smile and hold God's beauty
    Deep within your heart
Until our Lord comes again
    And from earth we do depart.

Joyce Hayes
Easton, Washington

MY BACKYARD

Today the March wind is pushing
huge cloud barges through
the blue, blue waters of my sky.
They hurry by my window
on their way to some far
place where the air is
still and calm.
But not for long as they
will soon arrive huffing and puffing,
blowing their message
of unsettled spring.

Coleen Y. Olson
Des Moines, Iowa

MORNING MAGIC

So early in the morning in the
    stillness of the dawn
When the dewdrops form a pattern
    so magnificently drawn,

When a hint of early sunbeams
    steals across the eastern sky
And all of earth's fair creatures
    still in tranquil slumber lie,

Now the cock his duty calling
    on the gatepost takes his stand
As his cry of all the ages
    he brings forth to wake the land.

The birds are stirring, twittering,
    each in its own accord.
Their throats swell with their chorus—
    another day is born!

Esther Schwartz
Geneva, Indiana

RAIN

rain
is like
a tear
when the earth gives birth
to Spring—and Nature
is a gilded wing
on the winds that sing
rain
is like
a tear

Velma M. Kubecki
Latrobe, Pennsylvania

A Walk

A walk. The atmosphere incredibly pure—a warm, caressing gentleness in the sunshine—joy in one's whole being. . . . Forgotten impressions of childhood and youth came back to me—all those indescribable effects wrought by color, shadow, sunlight, green hedges, and songs of birds, upon the soul just opening to poetry. I became again young, wondering, and simple, as candor and ignorance are simple. I abandoned myself to life and to nature, and they cradled me with an infinite gentleness. To open one's heart in purity to this ever pure nature, to allow this immortal life of things to penetrate into one's soul, is at the same time to listen to the voice of God. Sensation may be a prayer, and self-abandonment an act of devotion.

Henri Amiel

Journey through the garden gate to this tranquil abode on Nantucket Island, Massachusetts.
Photograph by William Johnson/Johnson's Photography.

HAPPINESS

If I might have one prayer, and one alone,
Granted for all the hearts I hold most dear
(Aside from the ultimate peace), I could make it known
In a brief petition—one word crystal-clear:
Happiness! God grant it now, I pray:
That shining thing within the human breast

Beech trees adorned with spring-green leaves shelter a woodland stream in Cotton Hollon Preserve, Glastonbury, Connecticut.
Photograph by William Johnson/Johnson's Photography.

With which men walk high-hearted all the way,
Without which there is never any rest.

Happiness! One brief and shining word,
Yet underlying it is all of good.
No heart is happy, quite, Thou knowest, Lord,
Unless beneath it life runs as it should:
A clear, clean, sparkling stream to heal and bless—
That radiance known to men as "happiness."

Grace Noll Crowell

~25~

A SLICE OF LIFE

Edgar A. Guest

THE EVENING PRAYER

Little daughter, kneeling there,
　　Speaking low your evening prayer,
In your cunning little nightie
　　With your pink toes peeping through,
With your eyes closed and your hands
　　Tightly clasped, while daddy stands
In the doorway, just to hear the
　　"God bless Papa," lisped by you,
You don't know just what I feel,
　　As I watch you nightly kneel
By your trundle bed and whisper

Soft and low your little prayer!
But in all I do or plan,
　　I'm a bigger, better man
Every time I hear you asking
　　God to make my journey fair.
Little daughter, kneeling there,
　　Lisping low your evening prayer,
Asking God above to bless me
　　At the closing of each day,
Oft the tears come to my eyes,
　　And I feel a big lump rise

McRAE

In my throat, that I can't swallow,
    And I sometimes turn away.
In the morning, when I wake,
    And my post of duty take,
I go forth with new-born courage
    To accomplish what is fair;
And, throughout the live-long day,
    I am striving every way
To come back to you each evening
    And be worthy of your prayer.

Two Prayers

Last night my little boy confessed to me
Some childish wrong;
And kneeling at my knee,
He prayed with tears—
"Dear God, make me a man
Like Daddy—wise and strong;
I know You can."

Then while he slept,
I knelt beside his bed,
Confessed my sins,
And prayed with low-bowed head.
"O God, make me a child
Like my child here—
Pure, guileless,
Trusting Thee with faith sincere."

Andrew Gillies

Mr. Sandman leads a drowsy little boy into dreamland. Photograph by Uniphoto.

SONG OF EASTER

Sing, children, sing!
And the lily censers swing;
Sing that life and joy are waking and that Death no more is king.
Sing the happy, happy tumult of the slowly brightening spring;
Sing, children, sing!

Sing, children, sing!
Winter wild has taken wing.
Fill the air with the sweet tidings till the frosty echoes ring!
Along the eaves the icicles no longer glittering cling;
And the crocus in the garden lifts its bright face to the Sun,
And in the meadows softly the brooks begin to run;
And the golden catkins swing
In the warm airs of the spring;
Sing, little children, sing!

Sing, little children, sing!
The lilies white you bring
In the joyous Easter morning for hope are blossoming;
And as the earth her shroud of snow from off her breast doth fling,
So may we cast our fetters off in God's eternal spring.
So may we find release at last from sorrow and from pain,
So may we find our childhood's calm, delicious dawn again.
Sweet are your eyes, O little ones, that look with smiling grace,
Without a shade of doubt or fear into the Future's face!
Sing, sing in happy chorus, with joyful voices tell
That death is life, and God is good, and all things shall be well;
That bitter days shall cease
In warmth and light and peace—
That winter yields to spring—
Sing, little children, sing!

Celia Thaxter

Devotions FROM THE Heart

Pamela Kennedy

"And they departed quickly from the sepulcher with fear and great joy; and did run to bring his disciples word."

Matthew 28:8

FEAR AND JOY

We recently moved—again. In the past twenty-eight years, we have moved eighteen times, so perhaps moving shouldn't be traumatic for our family. But there are always unknown aspects of new locations, schools, neighborhoods, even cultures that set our hearts to beating just a bit faster. Will the children adjust? Will we make friends quickly? Will we find good dentists and doctors and a beautician who knows how to cut my hair the way I like? Some of the concerns are big ones and others quite small, but they often join together to form a degree of fear that accompanies us to our new home. Mixed with that apprehension is another feeling equally as familiar; the anticipation and joy of discovery. For each new location holds, like an unopened gift, the promise of delightful surprises, exciting adventures, and enriching friendships.

As I reread the Easter story from Matthew's Gospel, I see that same mixture of fear and joy in the hearts of the women who hurried to the tomb that first Easter dawn. They were met, not with the expected rocky sepulcher containing the body of their Lord, but an angel who told them Jesus had risen and was headed to Galilee! Everything they knew about death and dying, about tombs and bodies, was turned upside down in that moment. They moved from a comfortable understanding about the world to a new and uncomfortable revelation that left them both fearful and filled with joy.

I believe their fear came from the changes that confronted them. What would happen now? Would anyone believe their experience with the angel?

Lord, help me to face the unknown path before me with joy, knowing You go before me each step of the way.

How would this new revelation alter their lives? These questions, just like mine about moving to a new location and all the readjustments involved in relocating our family, held a degree of fear because the answers were hidden. This was uncharted territory. But notice the women's fear was accompanied by joy. It was a joy driven by the information they received from the angel—"And go quickly, and tell his disciples that he (Jesus) is risen from the dead; and, behold, he goeth before you into Galilee; there shall ye see him" (Matthew 28:7).

Although I may not receive an angelic revelation, I can participate in the same joy these first-century believers experienced when I understand the truth that Jesus is still alive and He goes before me. Meditating on His comforting and encouraging presence, I need not fear the unknown future. True, I do not know what lies ahead, but I know the One who goes before me and waits for me there. My anxious expectations turn to bright hope as I trust in God to be present in my future as surely as He has been in my past. In His abiding strength and power I find the courage needed to face my future, to make new friends, to start a new job, to discover new abilities—even to find a new hairdresser!

Some of us may never move to a new location, but all of us experience changes that bring us face to face with the unknown. Understanding that God has already gone on ahead brings joy even in the midst of our fear. In that assurance we can start down the path before us just as the women did that long ago Easter morning when they hurried into their future, afraid, yet filled with joy.

Vibrant peonies and colorful foxglove say "welcome home" at this dwelling in Allentown, Pennsylvania. Photograph by D. Petku/H. Armstrong Roberts.

Through Mary's Eyes

I see Him working by my husband's side
    Within the shop where Joseph plies his trade;
And I, His mother, Mary, watch Him smile
    With satisfaction at some chair He's made.

I proudly marvel at His purity—
    The beauty of His glowing, godly face—
How quickly He has done each given task,
    His every movement rich in loving grace!

I watch Him cross the dark'ning room and pause
    Beside the moonlit window, looking out.
His lips move silently in prayer; He prays
    For that great work that He must be about.

O Jesus, once my tiny, blessed babe,
    How dearly I would hold You to me still,
And yet my heart must bid You leave this house
    That You may do Your heavenly Father's will!

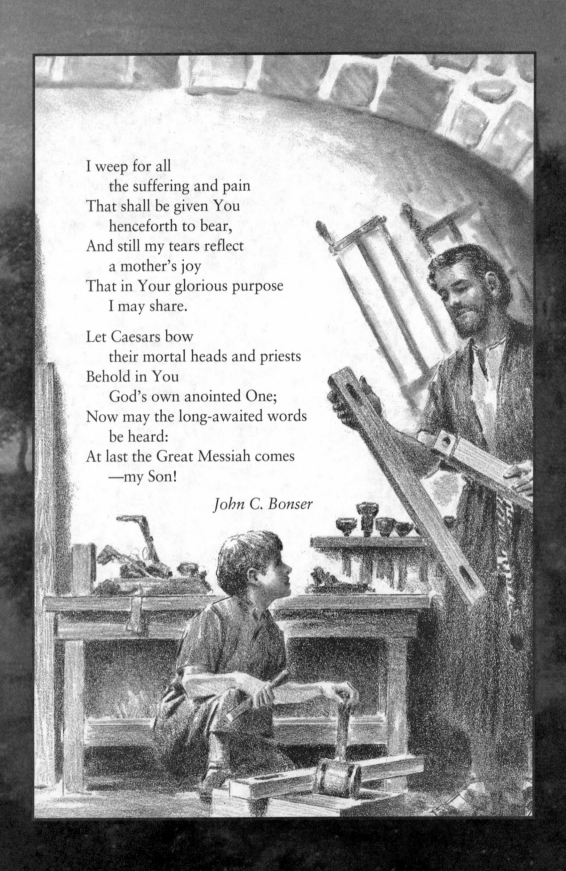

I weep for all
    the suffering and pain
That shall be given You
    henceforth to bear,
And still my tears reflect
    a mother's joy
That in Your glorious purpose
    I may share.

Let Caesars bow
    their mortal heads and priests
Behold in You
    God's own anointed One;
Now may the long-awaited words
    be heard:
At last the Great Messiah comes
    —my Son!

John C. Bonser

THE UPPER ROOM

And the first day of unleavened bread, when they killed the passover, his disciples said unto him, Where wilt thou that we go and prepare that thou mayest eat the passover?

And he sendeth forth two of his disciples, and saith unto them, Go ye into the city, and there shall meet you a man bearing a pitcher of water: follow him. And wheresoever he shall go in, say ye to the goodman of the house, The Master saith, Where is the guest chamber, where I shall eat the passover with my disciples? And he will shew you a large upper room furnished and prepared: there make ready for us.

And his disciples went forth, and came into the city, and found as he had said unto them: and they made ready the passover.

And in the evening he cometh with the twelve. And as they did eat, Jesus took bread, and blessed, and brake it, and gave to them, and said, Take, eat: this is my body.

And he took the cup, and when he had given thanks, he gave it to them: and they all drank of it. And he said unto them, This is my blood of the new testament, which is shed for many. Verily I say unto you, I will drink no more of the fruit of the vine, until that day that I drink it new in the kingdom of God.

MARK 14:12–17; 22–25

James J. Tissot (1836–1902) was a nineteenth-century French painter who favored religious themes in his work. A pupil of Flandrin and of Lamothe, Tissot is known for rendering intense facial expressions in his paintings, as seen in The Last Discourse of Our Lord Jesus Christ, opposite. Image courtesy of Superstock.

AGONY IN THE GARDEN

Then cometh Jesus with them unto a place called Gethsemane, and saith unto the disciples, Sit ye here, while I go and pray yonder.

And he took with him Peter and the two sons of Zebedee, and began to be sorrowful and very heavy.

Then saith he unto them, My soul is exceeding sorrowful, even unto death: tarry ye here, and watch with me.

And he went a little farther, and fell on his face, and prayed, saying, O my Father, if it be possible, let this cup pass from me: nevertheless not as I will, but as thou wilt.

And he cometh unto the disciples, and findeth them asleep, and saith unto Peter, What, could ye not watch with me one hour? Watch and pray, that ye enter not into temptation: the spirit indeed is willing, but the flesh is weak.

He went away again the second time, and prayed, saying, O my Father, if this cup may not pass away from me, except I drink it, thy will be done.

And he came and found them asleep again: for their eyes were heavy. And he left them, and went away again, and prayed the third time, saying the same words.

MATTHEW 26:36–44

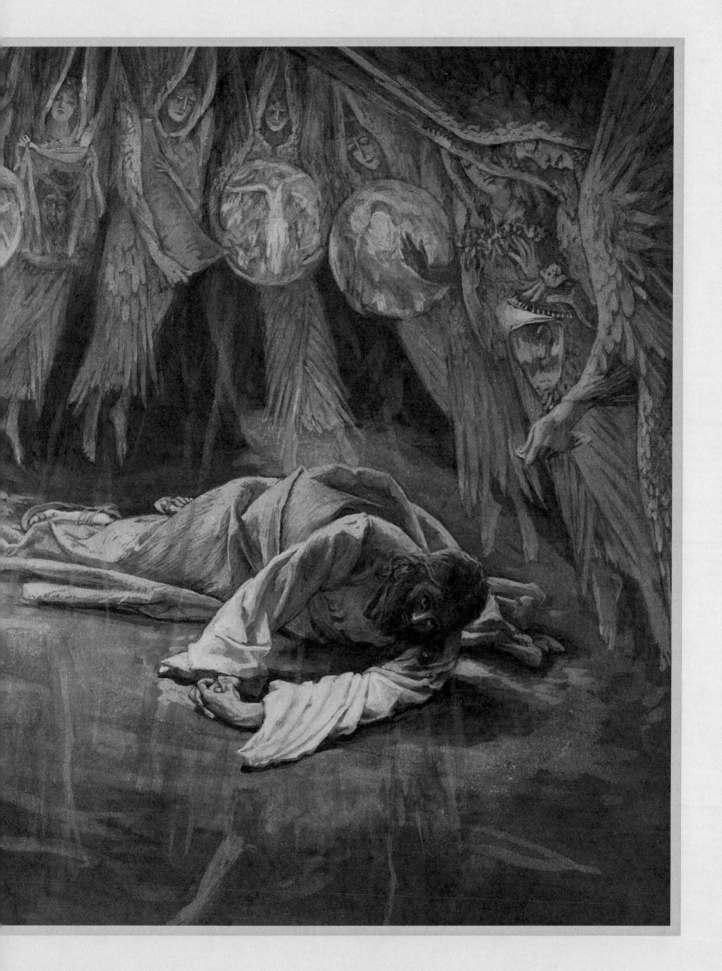

THE SON OF GOD

And Jesus cried with a loud voice, and gave up the ghost. And the veil of the temple was rent in twain from the top to the bottom.

And when the centurion, which stood over against him, saw that he so cried out, and gave up the ghost, he said, Truly this man was the Son of God.

There were also women looking on afar off: among whom was Mary Magdalene, and Mary the mother of James the less and of Joses, and Salome;

And now when the even was come, because it was the preparation, that is, the day before the sabbath, Joseph of Arimathaea, an honourable counsellor, which also waited for the kingdom of God, came, and went in boldly unto Pilate, and craved the body of Jesus.

And Pilate marvelled if he were already dead: and calling unto him the centurion, he asked him whether he had been any while dead. And when he knew it of the centurion, he gave the body to Joseph.

And he bought fine linen, and took him down, and wrapped him in the linen, and laid him in a sepulchre which was hewn out of a rock, and rolled a stone unto the door of the sepulchre.

MARK 15:37–40; 42–46

Woman, Behold Thy Son, Stabat Mater, *James J. Tissot (1836–1902). Image courtesy of Superstock.*

BE NOT AFRAID

Now upon the first day of the week, very early in the morning, they came unto the sepulchre, bringing the spices which they had prepared, and certain others with them.

And they found the stone rolled away from the sepulchre.

And they entered in, and found not the body of the Lord Jesus.

And it came to pass, as they were much perplexed thereabout, behold, two men stood by them in shining garments:

And as they were afraid, and bowed down their faces to the earth, they said unto them, Why seek ye the living among the dead?

He is not here, but is risen: remember how he spake unto you when he was yet in Galilee,

Saying, The Son of man must be delivered into the hands of sinful men, and be crucified, and the third day rise again.

And they departed quickly from the sepulchre with fear and great joy; and did run to bring his disciples word.

And as they went to tell his disciples, behold, Jesus met them, saying, All hail. And they came and held him by the feet, and worshipped him.

Then said Jesus unto them, Be not afraid: go tell my brethren that they go into Galilee, and there shall they see me.

LUKE 24:1–7
MATTHEW 28:8–10

Christ Appears to the Women, James J. Tissot (1836–1902).
Image courtesy of Superstock.

The Appearance to Mary

But Mary stood without at the sepulchre weeping: and as she wept, she stooped down, and looked into the sepulchre,

And seeth two angels in white sitting, the one at the head, and the other at the feet, where the body of Jesus had lain.

And they say unto her, Woman, why weepest thou? She saith unto them, Because they have taken away my Lord, and I know not where they have laid him.

And when she had thus said, she turned herself back, and saw Jesus standing, and knew not that it was Jesus.

Jesus saith unto her, Woman, why weepest thou? whom seekest thou? She, supposing him to be the gardener, saith unto him, Sir, if thou have borne him hence, tell me where thou hast laid him, and I will take him away.

Jesus saith unto her, Mary. She turned herself, and saith unto him, Rabboni; which is to say, Master.

Jesus saith unto her, Touch me not; for I am not yet ascended to my Father: but go to my brethren, and say unto them, I ascend unto my Father, and your Father; and to my God, and your God.

John 20:11–17

Noli Me Tangere, James J. Tissot (1836–1902). Image courtesy of Superstock.

THE ASCENSION

And he said unto them, These are the words which I spake unto you, while I was yet with you, that all things must be fulfilled, which were written in the law of Moses, and in the prophets, and in the psalms, concerning me.

Then opened he their understanding, that they might understand the scriptures,

And said unto them, Thus it is written, and thus it behoved Christ to suffer, and to rise from the dead the third day:

And that repentance and remission of sins should be preached in his name among all nations, beginning at Jerusalem.

And ye are witnesses of these things.

And, behold, I send the promise of my Father upon you: but tarry ye in the city of Jerusalem, until ye be endued with power from on high.

And he led them out as far as to Bethany, and he lifted up his hands, and blessed them. And it came to pass, while he blessed them, he was parted from them, and carried up into heaven.

And they worshipped him, and returned to Jerusalem with great joy: And were continually in the temple, praising and blessing God. Amen.

LUKE 24:44–53

Ascension from the Mount of Olives, James J. Tissot (1836–1902). Image courtesy of Superstock.

THROUGH MY WINDOW

Pamela Kennedy

Art by Patrick McRae

THOMAS, THE END OF DOUBTING

He wanted to be alone. For more than three years he had walked and talked, eaten and slept with the Master and the other disciples. Theirs had been a unity of diversity—fishermen, tax collector, accountant, zealot, schemers, dreamers— all bound together by the Word. They had left all they knew to follow One who knew all. And now Thomas needed to be by himself to think. Did any of it make sense now? Or was it all a delusion born of their mutual desire for redemption—a redemption of their belief that God cared about their world?

Alone on a rocky precipice overlooking the barren shoreline of the Salt Sea, Thomas raised his eyes in supplication. Who would answer his questions now? Who would satisfy the hunger that stabbed his soul? Slipping to his knees on the stony, hard-packed earth, he drew his cloak about him and retreated into memories.

He recalled the day he first heard of Jesus. There was such excitement in the small town where he lived! Some said a prophet walked the streets, healing the sick and driving out evil spirits. Others

claimed the long-awaited Messiah had arrived. Thomas did not want to hear what others thought, but rushed to the marketplace to see for himself. He followed at a distance, watching and listening. He saw lepers touched and cleansed, blind men given sight, a woman weak with fever restored to perfect health. And the words! Words of truth that gave form and reason to faith! This was a man Thomas could believe in. He was not another of the many impostors who regularly passed through the town relieving the citizens of their money and little else. And so, Thomas left his home and followed Jesus, hanging on His words, absorbing His presence, feeding on the Bread of Life.

The morning Jesus called together all His disciples and then chose twelve from among them, designating them as apostles, Thomas thought his heart would burst with joy. He was loved by the Master, chosen by name. He determined at that moment to follow without reservation and to give his very life if it were required to prove his devotion to God. He recalled how the others tried to dissuade Jesus from making the dangerous trip to Bethany at the request of Mary and Martha, and how he had cried, "Let us also go, that we may die with him." How bold and strong his faith had been. And when he heard Jesus' voice call out "Lazarus!" and saw with his own eyes the shrouded man walk from his tomb, Thomas knew the affirmation of his faith. There was no room for doubt in the burning light of that resurrection morning!

When Jesus gathered the dozen in the upper room and spoke of His departure to His Father's house, Thomas was confused. But when he asked how they could know the way to follow, Jesus looked at him in love and answered, "I am the way. . . ." Fears banished once again, Thomas looked to the future with confidence.

But then came the terror of the midnight arrest in the garden and the worse horror of the daylight when Jesus hung on the cross and died under the relentless Jerusalem sun. Thomas shuddered as he recalled the grief on Mary's face, the sobbing women, the mocking soldiers and taunting crowds. Where was the way now? How could he find it? He didn't want to be with the other apostles until he sorted out his confusion. So he left the city and came to this desolate place where the landscape matched his mood.

It was there in the wilderness that the others found him, weak and hungry, an emptiness in his eyes. In their excitement, they overlooked his disheveled appearance.

James grasped him by the shoulders, "You must come with us back to Jerusalem! The Master lives!"

Thomas stared at him as if he were mad.

"He lives! It's true!" added Philip. "We all saw Him, talked with Him! He wants to see you, Thomas. There's work for us yet in His kingdom. Come with us and see for yourself."

Thomas drew back from them then and stared at their faces in bewilderment. "Unless I see the nail marks in His hands and put my finger where the nails were and put my hand into His side, I will not believe it!" He spoke the last words with deliberate intensity, challenging them to question his resolve.

"Then come," John urged gently. "Come see for yourself what we have all witnessed. You are tired and you grieve, but I know you will find peace if you will just return with us to the upper room."

Exhausted, unwilling to resist their urging any longer, Thomas wrapped his cloak about him and followed his friends down the hillside back to the little house in Jerusalem. For several days he stayed with them in the locked room as they prayed and talked excitedly of the vision they had seen. He sat against the wall, an outsider, listening, but not partaking in their conversations. Their words droned on, rising and falling like the dust dancing in the afternoon sun. Then suddenly something was different, changed. The texture of the air seemed to alter and the apostles' words trailed off into silence. Thomas glanced up from his contemplation and caught his breath.

There, standing before him, was Jesus. "Peace be with you!" He said, and the words echoed in the tiny room like a rushing wind. Then the Master stood before Thomas, drawing him to his feet with the power of His presence. His eyes bore into the trembling disciple as if seeking his soul, and He spoke once more.

"Put your finger here; see my hands. Reach out your hand and put it into my side. Stop doubting and believe."

Thomas felt as if a sword had pierced his heart. He heard his own proud and defiant challenge turned back at him in compassion and love, and the pain of guilt tore at his soul. He recoiled from the outstretched hand that bore the marks of the executioner's spike; winced at the torn flesh of the Saviour's side, then fell prostrate on the floor. In wonder and shame he cried, "My Lord and my God!" How could he have doubted? How could he ever be forgiven for the weakness of his faith? He, who once had thought to die for Christ, could not even bear to look into His face.

And then the Lord gently touched him on the shoulder and raised him to his feet. As if in benediction Jesus rested His eyes on the anguished face of His disciple. "Because you have seen me, you have believed; blessed are those who have not seen and yet have believed."

They were not words of condemnation, but of challenge; and in that moment Thomas realized he had been given new hope and a commission. God was not finished with him yet. He would go, to the ends of the earth if necessary, and tell those he met that Christ was alive. They may not see, but through his testimony, empowered by the spirit of the living God, they would believe. And their belief would be his legacy—a legacy built not on doubt, but faith.

Pamela Kennedy is a freelance writer of short stories, articles, essays, and children's books. Wife of a retired naval officer and mother of three children, she has made her home on both U.S. coasts and currently resides in Kent, Washington.

EASTER DAY

Christ the Lord is risen today,
   Sons of men and angels say;
Raise your joys and triumphs high,
   Sing, ye heavens, and earth reply.

Love's redeeming work is done,
   Fought the fight, the victory won;
Jesus' agony is o'er,
   Darkness veils the earth no more.

Vain the stone, the watch, the seal,
   Christ hath burst the gates of hell;
Death in vain forbids Him rise,
   Christ hath opened Paradise.

Soar we now where Christ hath led,
   Following our exalted Head;
Made like Him, like Him to rise;
   Ours the cross, the grave, the skies.

Charles Wesley

AN EASTER CANTICLE

In every trembling bud and bloom
    That cleaves the earth, a flowery sword,
I see Thee come from out the tomb,
    Thou risen Lord.

Thou art not dead! Thou art the whole
    Of life that quickens in the sod;
Green April is Thy very soul,
    Thou great Lord God.

Charles Hanson Towne

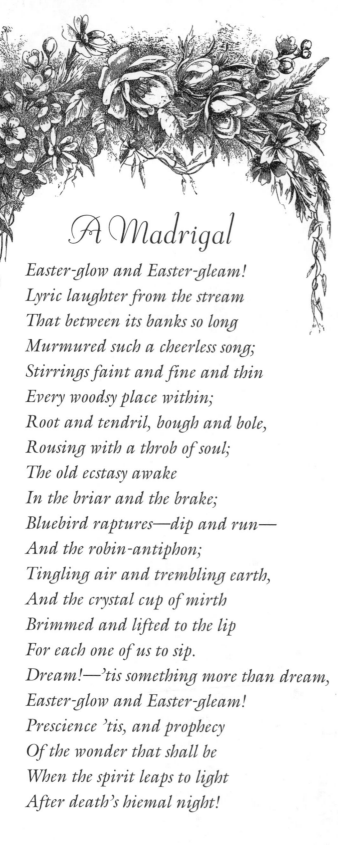

A Madrigal

Easter-glow and Easter-gleam!
Lyric laughter from the stream
That between its banks so long
Murmured such a cheerless song;
Stirrings faint and fine and thin
Every woodsy place within;
Root and tendril, bough and bole,
Rousing with a throb of soul;
The old ecstasy awake
In the briar and the brake;
Bluebird raptures—dip and run—
And the robin-antiphon;
Tingling air and trembling earth,
And the crystal cup of mirth
Brimmed and lifted to the lip
For each one of us to sip.
Dream!—'tis something more than dream,
Easter-glow and Easter-gleam!
Prescience 'tis, and prophecy
Of the wonder that shall be
When the spirit leaps to light
After death's hiemal night!

Clinton Scollard

Blossoming cherry trees adorn Phelps Creek in the Columbia River Gorge National Scenic Area, Oregon. Photograph by Steve Terrill.

Real

"What is real?" asked the Rabbit one day. "Does it mean having things that buzz inside you and a stick-out handle?"

"Real isn't how you are made," said the Skin Horse. "It's a thing that happens to you. When a child loves you for a long, long time, not just to play with, but *really* loves you, then you become Real."

"Does it hurt?" asked the Rabbit.

"Sometimes," said the Skin Horse, for he was always truthful. "When you are Real you don't mind being hurt."

"Does it happen all at once, like being wound up," he asked, "or bit by bit?"

"It doesn't happen all at once," said the Skin Horse. "You become. It takes a long time. That's why it doesn't often happen to people who break easily, or have sharp edges, or who have to be carefully kept. Generally, by the time you are Real, most of your hair has been loved off, and your eyes drop out and you get loose in the joints and very shabby. But these things don't matter at all, because once you are Real you can't be ugly, except to people who don't understand."

Margery Williams
from The Velveteen Rabbit

A child's playmate waits patiently for his best friend's return. Photograph by Jessie Walker.

HANDMADE HEIRLOOM

Recycled fabric scraps become handmade rag baskets to treasure. Photo by Allan Newman/The Newman O'Neill Group, Inc.
From Family Circle Weekend Crafts published by Collier Newfield, Inc. © 1989 by Collier Newfield, Inc. All rights reserved.

RAG BASKETS
Caroline Rankin

My first child was born a year ago, in the springtime. It was a soft and warm April day, the kind of day that hints at the glorious weather to come, even if it can't promise that winter's snows are finished for the year. And, of course, they weren't. Before my daughter was a week old, winter's last gasp covered our yard with eight inches of heavy, wet snow, the kind that brings down tree limbs and power lines and makes driving nearly impossible. "Welcome to life in Vermont," I whispered in her ear as we sat in our rocking chair by the window and watched the thick, white flakes fall.

And now we have watched a full cycle of the seasons from our window. My daughter is one year old—and although her first birthday brought damp, raw weather, it once again had an unmistakable flavor of spring, for it fell on Easter Sunday. I chose to mark the day with a very special gift, a beautiful

~56~

handmade Easter basket that I hope will bring the breath of spring to her life for years to come.

My basket combines two ancient crafts: rag work and basketry. Years ago, I inherited from my own mother the habit of saving old clothes whose functional lives were finished but whose fabric still held promise. My mother used to make braided rugs, a skill she learned from her grandmother. I too have made my share of rugs, braided as well as hooked, from my own fabric collection. But a few years back I became enamored of basketry and put my trunk of fabric scraps aside. Happily, this rag basket project combines my old love with the new.

Basketry is as old as civilization. Every culture in every corner of the world has developed its own uses for and styles of baskets. They have been made from grasses, reeds, stems, barks, roots, vines, leaves, corn husks, and more. They have been used for storage, for measuring, for cooking, for transporting, and for cradling babies. The history of the craft is too vast to summarize. Suffice it to say that baskets have been an essential part of life for centuries; and like most handmade items that begin as utilitarian objects, they soon became objects of art, reflecting the culture and personality of their makers in the details of their shapes, design, and technique.

Crafting with rags may not be as ancient an art, but it is of a similar nature. Rag work has simple, utilitarian roots. Long before we were recycling for environmental reasons, people were recycling to make the most of limited resources. Old fabric found new life in rugs that warmed and insulated dwellings. Hooked rugs appear to be the most ancient variety of rag rugs. Braided rugs became prevalent in nineteenth-century New England and still add immeasurable charm and warmth to a home. Today's crafters are making rugs and more from fabric scraps, recycling the old into something new using traditional hooking and braiding techniques as well as knitting, crocheting, and wrapping.

The coiled basket I decided to make for a birth-

> *Years ago, I inherited from my own mother the habit of saving old clothes whose functional lives were finished but whose fabric still held promise.*

day and Easter basket for my daughter draws upon both these ancient traditions to make a beautiful, heirloom-quality craft. The materials are basic: several spools of half-inch wide jute, sisal, or craft cord; a collection of fabric scraps cut into one-inch strips, and a large-eyed, blunt-end tapestry needle. The technique is tricky to describe but actually quite simple to carry out. The basket is made from one continuous coil, beginning at the center of the bottom. The idea is to create a spiral, connecting one ring of cord to the next by wrapping the cord with fabric strips in a figure-eight pattern. The spiral is made flat to form the basket bottom, and then angled up and slightly outward to shape the body. The handle is wrapped separately, and then attached with the fabric strips to the top of the basket. Look for craft books on both rag work and basketry that describe the coiling and wrapping technique. Once the basics become clear, the basket is quite easy to complete.

I used some of my old collection of fabric scraps to make my basket, but the bulk of my material came from some of my daughter's discarded baby clothes. Any mother knows that in a year of life a child can go through a dresser full of clothes, and some are simply too worn or too stained to hand down to a future sibling, yet still too precious to throw away. On that wonderful—albeit cold and wet—Easter Sunday birthday morning, I filled my basket with tiny, soft stuffed animals, two baby board books, and a bag of homemade butter cookies. My daughter delighted in removing each item and in carrying the basket about the house by its handle. The soft fabric was a good match for her little, plump hands, and the basket proved sturdy through rough treatment. My dear little one knows nothing of basketry or rag-work, nothing of ancient crafts or modern innovations, but she does know the soft, warm feeling of her mother's love. Someday her basket can serve as a symbol of these delightful days which she will not remember, but which will certainly leave their impression upon her life.

Ideals:
Family Recipes

Do you find yourself on Easter Sunday with dozens of left-over hard-boiled eggs? To help with this annual problem, here are some creative solutions provided by Ideals readers from across the country.

Confetti Potato Salad

4 medium potatoes, halved
4 green onions, thinly sliced
½ cup chopped green pepper
1 stalk celery, thinly sliced
1 small carrot, grated
2 to 3 pimiento-stuffed olives

2 hard-boiled eggs, chopped
½ cup sour cream
1 tablespoon lemon juice
1 teaspoon dillweed
Lettuce leaves
Paprika

Place the potatoes in a large saucepan; add water to cover. Bring water to a boil; continue boiling 20 minutes or until potatoes are tender. Drain. Allow potatoes to cool; cut into cubes.

In a large bowl, combine potatoes, green onions, green pepper, celery, carrot, olives, and eggs. Set aside. In a small bowl, combine sour cream, lemon juice, and dillweed. Stir well. Add dressing to potato mixture and toss gently. Salt to taste. Serve on lettuce leaves; sprinkle with paprika. Makes 5 to 6 servings.

Mrs. Lydia Miller
Garnett, Kansas

Curried Egg Salad Spread

¼ cup mayonnaise
½ teaspoon Worcestershire sauce
1 teaspoon curry powder
¼ teaspoon salt

¼ teaspoon pepper
8 water chestnuts, chopped
6 hard-boiled eggs, chopped
2 green onions, chopped

In a large bowl, combine mayonnaise, Worcestershire sauce, curry powder, salt, and pepper. Stir well. Add water chestnuts, eggs, and green onions; stir well. Cover and chill until ready to serve. Makes about 2 cups.

Michelle Parker
Fresno, California

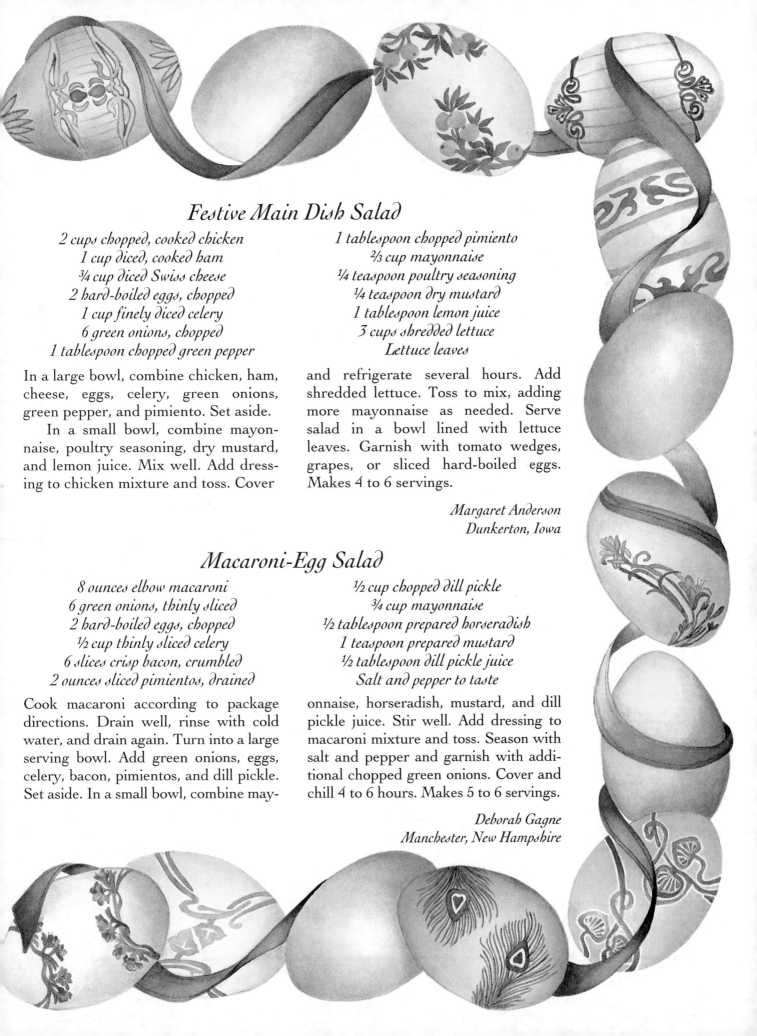

Festive Main Dish Salad

2 cups chopped, cooked chicken
1 cup diced, cooked ham
¾ cup diced Swiss cheese
2 hard-boiled eggs, chopped
1 cup finely diced celery
6 green onions, chopped
1 tablespoon chopped green pepper

1 tablespoon chopped pimiento
⅔ cup mayonnaise
¼ teaspoon poultry seasoning
¼ teaspoon dry mustard
1 tablespoon lemon juice
3 cups shredded lettuce
Lettuce leaves

In a large bowl, combine chicken, ham, cheese, eggs, celery, green onions, green pepper, and pimiento. Set aside.

In a small bowl, combine mayonnaise, poultry seasoning, dry mustard, and lemon juice. Mix well. Add dressing to chicken mixture and toss. Cover and refrigerate several hours. Add shredded lettuce. Toss to mix, adding more mayonnaise as needed. Serve salad in a bowl lined with lettuce leaves. Garnish with tomato wedges, grapes, or sliced hard-boiled eggs. Makes 4 to 6 servings.

Margaret Anderson
Dunkerton, Iowa

Macaroni-Egg Salad

8 ounces elbow macaroni
6 green onions, thinly sliced
2 hard-boiled eggs, chopped
½ cup thinly sliced celery
6 slices crisp bacon, crumbled
2 ounces sliced pimientos, drained

½ cup chopped dill pickle
¾ cup mayonnaise
½ tablespoon prepared horseradish
1 teaspoon prepared mustard
½ tablespoon dill pickle juice
Salt and pepper to taste

Cook macaroni according to package directions. Drain well, rinse with cold water, and drain again. Turn into a large serving bowl. Add green onions, eggs, celery, bacon, pimientos, and dill pickle. Set aside. In a small bowl, combine mayonnaise, horseradish, mustard, and dill pickle juice. Stir well. Add dressing to macaroni mixture and toss. Season with salt and pepper and garnish with additional chopped green onions. Cover and chill 4 to 6 hours. Makes 5 to 6 servings.

Deborah Gagne
Manchester, New Hampshire

PUSS, TINEY, AND BESS

In the year 1774, being much indisposed both in mind and body, incapable of diverting myself either with company or books, and yet in a condition that made some diversion necessary, I was glad of any thing that would engage my attention without fatiguing it. The children of a neighbour of mine had a leveret given them for a plaything; it was at that time about three months old. Understanding better how to tease the poor creature than to feed it, and soon becoming weary of their charge, they readily consented that their father, who saw it pining and growing leaner every day, should offer it to my acceptance. I was willing enough to take the prisoner under my protection, perceiving that in the management of such an animal, and in the attempt to tame it, I should find just that sort of employment which my case required. It was soon known among the neighbours that I was pleased with the present, and the consequence was, that in a short time I had as many leverets offered to me as would have stocked a paddock. I undertook the care of three. . . .

Puss grew presently familiar, would leap into my lap, raise himself upon his hinder feet, and bite the hair from my temples. He would suffer me to take him up and to carry him about in my arms, and has more than once fallen asleep upon my knee. He was ill three days, during which time I nursed him, kept him apart from his fellows that they might not molest him (for, like many other wild animals, they persecute one of their own species that is sick), and by constant care and trying him with a variety of herbs, restored him to perfect health. No creature could be more grateful than my patient after his recovery; a sentiment which he most significantly expressed, by licking my hand, first the back of it, then the palm, then every finger separately, then between all the fingers, as if anxious to leave no part of it unsaluted; a ceremony which he never performed but once again upon a similar occasion. Finding him extremely tractable, I made it my custom to carry him always after breakfast into the garden, where he hid himself generally under the leaves of a cucumber vine, sleeping or chewing the cud till evening; in the leaves also of that vine he found a favourite repast. I had not long habituated him to this taste of liberty, before he began to be impatient for the return of the time when he might enjoy it. He would invite me to the garden by drumming upon my knee, and by a look of such expression as it was not possible to misinterpret. If this rhetoric did not immediately succeed, he would take the skirt of my coat between his teeth, and pull at it with all his force. Thus Puss might be said to be perfectly tamed, the shyness of his nature was done away, and on the whole it was visible, by many symptoms which I have not room to enumerate, that he was happier in human society than when shut up with his natural companions. . . .

Puss is still living, and has just completed his tenth year, discovering no signs of decay, nor even of age, except that he is grown more discreet and less frolicksome than he was. I cannot conclude, without observing that I have lately introduced a dog to his acquaintance, a spaniel that had never seen a hare to a hare that had never seen a spaniel. I did it with great caution, but there was no real need of it. Puss discovered no token of fear, nor Marquis the least symptom of hostility. There is therefore, it should seem, no natural antipathy between dog and hare, but the pursuit of the one occasions the flight of the other, and the dog pursues because he is trained to it; they eat bread at the same time out of the same hand, and are in all respects sociable and friendly.

William Cowper

"Buck" stops to smell the flowers in the garden. Photograph by Superstock.

MUSIC AND THE SEA

When music spills from golden throat
In wild bird reveille,
I push the drab world out in space
And live in melody.
When color glows in countless ways
Before my hungry eyes,
I am a gourmand at the feast
Unmindful of how time flies,
For when this pageantry is spread
I quite forget my daily bread.

When cool waves run to greet the sands
And whisper deep-sea lore,
I stand, at crimson close of day,
Enchanted on the shore . . .
Each season wafts in new delights
As beauty flames its way,
On rock, and earth, and sky, and sea,
With respite for the day—
And oh, my dear, I humbly own
I cannot live by bread alone!

E. T. Scoville

*Earth and ocean
seem to sleep in
one another's arms
and dream.*

– Percy Bysshe Shelley

Early morning light washes the sea in water-colored, pastel shades at Julia Pfeiffer Burns State Park in Big Sur, California. Photograph by Dick Dietrich Photography.

Collector's Corner

Scrimshaw

by Anne Ferguson

For a child growing up near the sea, it is nearly impossible to imagine the life of an inland boy or girl. As elemental as the earth and the sky, the ocean shapes life along the seacoast. I was such a child of the sea. I measured my summers by long, sun-drenched days swimming in the icy cold waters near my Massachusetts home. I walked to school past stately sea captains' mansions that looked out over our harbor. I waited for the cooling sea breezes that offered relief on steamy July nights, and I watched the waves crash against sea walls during the stormy days of early fall. I pitied cousins whose parents had moved them to Ohio; I wondered what they would do all summer and how they would find their way around in a place where land stretched in every direction. And then I grew up, got married, and moved to Tennessee, a state with its share of natural beauty, but most definitively without an ocean view. There I came to realize that life goes on quite happily for the landlocked; but I also began collecting scrimshaw. I understand now that these small pieces of carved whalebone came to symbolize the life I had left behind but of which I wasn't willing to let go.

When I moved south so many years ago, I took with me the one piece of scrimshaw I owned, a yellowed whale's tooth with an intricate carving of a whaling ship and the inscription, "To my dear Lucy." The piece had been in my parents' home for years. Before I moved, I claimed the tooth—something familiar, a piece of home. But it wasn't until I was settled in Nashville that I took real notice of it. Only months into my new life and wallowing in homesickness, I picked up the carved tooth and began to think of home. Before long I was dropping into antique shops on visits home and looking for more scrimshaw. I started reading about the art, about the history of the whaling industry, about the sailors who whiled away idle hours on board ship by carving designs into whalebone and teeth. Like the tooth I already had, I discovered, many scrimshaw pieces were carved with a special woman in mind—a mother, a wife, a daughter, someone the sailor missed during the journeys that often lasted three years and more. I was hooked: a homesick New Englander washed up in Tennessee, I soon became an avid scrimshaw collector.

Today on my shelf, along with Lucy's tooth, are two other carved whale teeth, one with an amazingly detailed map of Nantucket Island and another which depicts a ship in pursuit of a whale. I also have some of the practical items made by scrimshanders: two pie jaggers, a sewing box, and a handful of carved busks—pieces of bone shaped into stays for a woman's corset. My collection is humble, no doubt; it is more a quiet oasis of memory than anything else. After more than two decades in Tennessee, after raising my family here and coming to think of this once strange southern place as home, I still miss the seacoast life of my childhood. No number of years can change the fact that my early days were shaped by the waters of the Atlantic. When I hold my scrimshaw pieces in my hands, the romance of the sea comes alive to me: I can hear the sea gulls, feel the rhythm of the waves, smell the moist salt air, and, most of all, I can imagine a bond with those long ago artisan sailors who missed their homes on land much in the way I still sometimes miss my home by the sea.

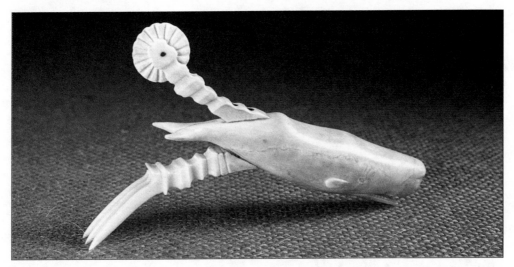

This antique scrimshaw jagging wheel was used for crimping the edges of pastries. Courtesy of Winterthur Museum, Delaware.

A BONE TO PICK
If you would like to start a scrimshaw collection, here are some interesting facts:

HISTORY
• An indigenous North American folk art, scrimshaw was popularized by New England sailors of the nineteenth century but is believed to have originated with Eskimos.

• The most likely root of the word *scrimshaw* is the Dutch word *skrimshander* meaning "idle fellow," which referred to the sailors who filled the idle hours on board ship carving whalebone.

• Although whaling was pursued by North American sailors from about 1700 until after 1900, the peak of the whaling industry in America was the mid-nineteenth century. In 1846, more than 800 ships sailed in the American whaling fleet; by 1912, there were fewer than ten, due in great part to the depleted whale population.

• An estimated 20,000 sailors tried their hand at scrimshaw during the whaling era in America. The earliest known written reference to scrimshaw dates to March 14, 1821.

• President John F. Kennedy's interest in scrimshaw sparked a boom in collecting in the late 1960s and early 1970s.

MATERIALS
Whalebone or whale teeth
Walrus or elephant tusks
Hippopotamus teeth

Coloring inks made from India ink, lamp-black, soot, tobacco juice, or berry juice

POPULAR ITEMS
Busks (corset stays)
Jagging wheels (pastry rollers)
Bodkins (sailors' needles)
Walking sticks and canes
Decorative teeth (prized by collectors)
Sewing boxes and thimbles

CAUTIONS FOR COLLECTORS
• The whale is protected today by the Endangered Species Act of 1973 and the Marine Mammal Protection Act of 1972, both of which put restrictions on the sale and importation of whalebone and teeth. Seek out reputable dealers for advice on identifying authentic and legal pieces.

• Fake scrimshaw exists in great quantities. Carved on polymer plastic, these copies can be identified by dealers with a heat test. True bone will not melt under a hot needle, while plastic will.

• Scrimshaw artisans today use the same methods perfected by the nineteenth-century sailors. Modern artisans can carve on whale-bone or teeth only if the material is certified as having been obtained before the Endangered Species Act.

Seashell

One day upon the beach I found
    A seashell washed ashore,
And as I put it to my ear,
    I heard the oceans roar.
It murmured of the storms at sea
    That surged with untold might
And whispered too of tropic islands
    Filled with rare delight.
I wondered how it came my way
    From deep within the sea
To nestle safely in my hand
    And sing these songs to me.
Adventure seemed to beckon as
    I held the lovely shell
And listened to the wondrous tales
    Of magic it did tell.
I took it home and placed it on
    A shelf where it could be
My ship of dreams that always held
    The music of the sea.

LaVerne P. Larson

Seashell treasures adorn antique linen. Photograph by D. Petku/H. Armstrong Roberts.

An ocean liner sets out for the high seas. Photograph by Randa Bishop/Uniphoto Picture Agency.

TRAVELER'S
Diary

Many women throughout the past century have traveled the continent and written captivating prose about their experiences. Here is an excerpt from the Canadian writer Edna Jaques's autobiography Uphill All the Way, *in which she describes her experiences working on a ship after World War I.*

from I BECOME A SAILOR
Edna Jaques

I boarded the train for Vancouver, and like the Israelites of old, not knowing whither they went, I arrived in the biggest city I had ever been in, and went to the Y.W.C.A. where I got a room, and didn't know what I would do next.

But on the train, sitting across the aisle from me, were a mother and her young daughter. We talked back and forth and they too went to stay at the "Y."

I had told them how I was looking forward to my first view of the ocean and next morning we three went down to the dock. I asked them to take my arm and lead me down the last block with my eyes shut, so the glory of the sea might burst on me all at once, which they laughingly did. When we were about halfway down, they said, "Now you can open your eyes," and what did I see: the great harbor as far as you could see from either side, one mass of ships, big ocean liners, coastal steamers, little fishing boats, all white and glinting in the sun, as if in answer to my wildest dream. And before me there was a blue sparkling sea, a thousand times more beautiful than I had ever imagined it.

I thanked them and went back to the Y.W.C.A. and said to the woman at the desk, "Oh, I wish I was a boy and then I could work on a boat." She said, "Well, you know, you don't have to be a boy now; there is one boat, the *Princess Adelaide*, that is hiring girls. There's a strike on and they are using girls."

I said goodbye and started on the run back to the dock, down the sloping run to the ship. There was a man standing there, a tall nice looking man, and I said, "I hear you are hiring girls to work on the boat." And he said, "We are." I gasped out, "Will you take me?" He laughed and said, "I will, you Irish giant. . . . Can you be back in a half-hour?" I yelled, "Sure," and ran back to the Y.W.C.A., got my grip and started on the run. I didn't know enough to take a street car. I arrived just as the whistle blew, and Mr. Allen smiled and said, "On with you. One of the girls will tell you where to go." Thus began the happiest year of my life.

It was called the "triangle run"—Vancouver, Victoria, and Seattle—six days a week. We left Vancouver around 10:30 A.M., went to Victoria sailing through one of the most beautiful seas in the world, through the "narrows"—the boat would rock in the meetings of the tides—around little stormy islands. Sometimes it seemed we would almost hit them, but the stout little ship with Captain Hunter standing staunch as a soldier in his little glassed-in lookout, giving his orders to the men far below, eased along with hardly a ripple, until we came around the last bend and headed into the open sea to Victoria.

There were fourteen of us, nice decent girls. They had partitioned off the rear end of the lower deck with a huge canvas for us, just above the propeller rod. Sometimes in the night on the run from Seattle to Vancouver, I would wake up to the steady beating of the propeller quietly turning and driving us along. It sounded soothing, like a heart beating in the night.

Each girl had a narrow cot, a little bureau and a rack for her clothes. Here we could wash out small underclothing, iron our uniforms, put our hair in curlers. We were safe and protected, and if Bill, the night watchman, had ever caught

a curious passenger trying to get a glimpse of us through a slit in the canvas, Bill would have thrown him overboard, I am sure.

How we enjoyed it, the companionship and the comfort, the happy laughter that always seemed to be there. I never met a nicer lot of girls, and Captain Hunter was proud as a peacock of us; in a kind of fatherly way, he took care of us all.

Each girl had eight staterooms to make up every morning. For me, being short, making those upper berths was surely hard. Now and then a tall girl would give me a hand, but as a rule I stood on a chair to make them up and as far as I know there were no complaints.

Each girl had her table also, where we waited on about eight people three times a day. How we stood it, I will never know. We worked fifteen hours a day, ate three big meals, slept the minute we hit the pillow and were as happy as clams. . . .

We would serve dinner from about five to eight and arrive in Seattle at nine P.M. Sometimes, when there wouldn't be too many passengers, we would finish early, and in order to fill in an hour or so until time to dock, a few of us younger girls would gather on the lower deck at the back and begin to sing. Maybe two or three baggage boys would join us. One of them had a guitar and as the boat moved along in the still moonlight, there would be a lovely air of happiness among us, with the beauty of the night and the long swells of the sea as it rolled in from deep water and struck the high white cliffs of Washington.

I can remember the cliffs as the moonlight hit them, shining and white against the darkness of the sea and sky, and then we would feel the quiet slowing down of the propellers as we came closer in. Then would come the shouting and running feet and the crew getting ready to unload; the spell would be broken, and work started again.

After an hour-and-a-half in Seattle, we would go down to our "glory hole," slip into our cots and be asleep in five minutes, safe and warm and strangely at home as the boat plowed its way back to its home port of Vancouver.

OLD IRONSIDES

Oliver Wendell Holmes

Ay, tear her tattered ensign down!
    Long has it waved on high,
And many an eye has danced to see
    That banner in the sky;
Beneath it rung the battle shout,
    And burst the cannon's roar;—
The meteor of the ocean air
    Shall sweep the clouds no more!

Her deck, once red with heroes' blood,
    Where knelt the vanquished foe,
When winds were hurrying o'er the flood,
    And waves were white below,

No more shall feel the victor's tread,
    Or know the conquered knee;—
The harpies of the shore shall pluck
    The eagle of the sea!

Oh, better that her shattered hulk
    Should sink beneath the wave;
Her thunders shook the mighty deep,
    And there should be her grave;
Nail to the mast her holy flag,
    Set every threadbare sail,
And give her to the god of storms,
    The lightning and the gale!

The U.S.S. Constitution sets sail in Boston Harbor during an anniversary celebration Parade of Sail.
Photography by William Johnson/Johnson's Photography.

ABOUT THE POEM

When nineteenth-century American poet Oliver Wendell Holmes picked up the newspaper and read that the Navy Department planned to demolish the U.S.S. Constitution, the famous frigate which served America in the War of 1812, he furiously composed a poem of protest. "Old Ironsides" garnered such a wealth of support from the public that the secretary of the Navy eventually countermanded the condemnation order and the U.S.S. Constitution was saved. The ship was later rebuilt in order that Americans could visit this floating symbol of freedom.

JACQUELINE COCHRAN

In her lifetime, pilot Jackie Cochran won more than two hundred aviation awards and achieved a list of firsts that rivals that of any pilot, male or female, in the history of aviation. She was the first woman to fly in the prestigious Bendix Trophy Transcontinental Race in 1934 and the first, four years later, to win that race. She was the first woman to pilot a bomber across the Atlantic Ocean in 1941; and in 1945, she received the Distinguished Service Medal, the first woman so honored, for her work to organize and run the Women's Air Force Service Pilots (WASP) during World War II. In 1953, Cochran flew faster than the speed of sound, the first woman to do so, and became one of only a handful of pilots of either gender to have achieved that milestone. Without question, Cochran's is an aviator's résumé with few equals; nonetheless, it may be that her greatest achievement had nothing at all to do with piloting or aviation. Jackie Cochran marked herself as special long before she had even dreamed of flying an airplane. At the age of eight, she found the courage to take responsibility for her own life and took the first step toward making something truly extraordinary out of the meager beginnings life had offered her.

·Jacqueline Cochran was born in 1910 in Pensacola, Florida. An orphan, she spent her early years with a foster family who scraped together an existence in a one-room shack on the edge of a swamp with no running water and no electricity. Cochran's foster family offered her a bed on their dirt floor and what food and clothing they could, but gave her little in the way of warmth, affection, or encouragement. Jackie attended less than two full years of school before her family's poverty convinced her to accept a local woman's offer of a job as a mother's helper earning ten cents a day. Jackie was eight years old, and never again would she rely upon anyone but herself for support.

It would be another fourteen years before Cochran first set foot in the cockpit of an airplane. In that time she worked long hours as a laborer, a housekeeper, a beauty shop assistant, and a nurse. Wherever she went she took with her a habit for hard work and optimism and a knack for attracting the attention of people in a position to help her along life's path. Cochran did not look for handouts, but rather for opportunities; and she never failed to rise to the challenge when presented with a chance to better herself. She was working twelve-hour shifts in a mill when she talked her way into her first position in a beauty shop, and she took up nursing after a customer in the beauty shop noticed her compassionate ways and offered to help her get started in nursing school. Through these years Cochran nurtured two complimentary goals: she wanted to raise herself out of the poverty of her childhood, and she wanted to find a way to help others who faced life in similar circumstances.

.Cochran had these two goals in mind when, at just twenty-two years old, she excitedly described to the man seated next to her at a dinner party the type of business she hoped to run someday—a cosmetics company with outlets all across the country. The man's name was Floyd Odlum, and he himself was a wealthy and respected businessman. He jokingly replied that to manage such a company, Cochran would need to have wings. Cochran agreed. She liked the idea. She liked it so much that she took Odlum seriously and decided to learn to fly. The woman who would one day become one of the greatest pilots in American history then proceeded to earn her license to fly during a three-week vacation from her job at a New York beauty salon.

Flying was what Cochran had been looking for all her life. It was the ultimate escape from the very earthbound poverty of her youth. Floyd Odlum eventually became her husband, and with his encouragement Cochran did manage to build the cosmetics company she had envisioned, and to help people in whom she saw a reflection of what she had once been—poor, alone, and struggling. But it was flying that consumed Jackie Cochran from 1932 on. In the 30s, when women pilots were few and far between, she got involved with air racing, a sport reluctant to accept women, but unable to deny the insistent and talented Cochran. She also became involved with the testing of aviation equipment. In later years, she would count this among her proudest achievements, for her work helped make planes safer and more efficient and helped air travel transform American life.

When World War II began, Cochran longed to get involved, but found opportunities for women pilots nearly non-existent. In 1941, however, General Hap Arnold of the U.S. Air Force invited Cochran to become the first woman pilot to help transport American planes overseas for use by the British in their war against Hitler. Soon after Cochran made her historic first bomber flight, Arnold asked her to stay in England and help organize British women pilots to help in the war effort. Cochran's British pilots transported equipment and moved planes under her supervision, until the U.S. entered the war and General Arnold called Cochran home. Now she took on her greatest challenge—organizing a women's branch of the air force. Under Cochran, the Women's Air Force Service Pilots trained and enlisted one thousand women to support the defense of the nation. Cochran's work with the WASPs won her the prestigious Distinguished Service Medal, and it also proved to a doubtful public that women had the courage, the stamina, and the ability to fly. After the war, Cochran saw that jets had become the aircraft of the future, and she trained to be a jet test pilot. It was in this capacity that she worked to break the speed of sound, doing so in 1953 despite the countless male pilots who guaranteed the feat was beyond the capacity of a woman.

Jackie Cochran continued to fly and to support flying for the remainder of her life. She died in 1980. In the Aviation Hall of Fame in Dayton, Ohio, her name and her long list of accomplishments are displayed among the elite of American flight. For a pilot, Cochran's story is a true inspiration, for she loved flying more than anything else in the world, and she gave the profession every ounce of her commitment and energy. But even for those of us with feet firmly planted on the ground, her story holds a lesson. Jackie Cochran was a woman of courage, character, and strength who found her life's calling in flying, but found the key to success in life long before she even laid eyes upon an airplane. From the age of eight, Cochran worked hard to support and better herself, deterred neither by bitterness over the hardships she had to overcome nor doubts about her own abilities. "What I have done," she wrote in her autobiography, "others can do also." Of course, Cochran did not mean that we could all fly a jet at the speed of sound; she simply knew from experience that when we take responsibility for our own lives, when we resist bitterness and regret and look for opportunities and not excuses, the sky is truly the limit.

Nancy Skarmeas is a book editor and mother of a toddler, Gordon, who is keeping her and her husband quite busy at their home in New Hampshire. Her Greek and Irish ancestry has fostered a lifelong interest in research and history.

A DAY OF SUNSHINE

O gift of God! O perfect day:
Whereon shall no man work, but play;
Whereon it is enough for me,
Not to be doing, but to be!

Through every fibre of my brain,
Through every nerve, through every vein,
I feel the electric thrill, the touch
Of life, that seems almost too much.

I hear the wind among the trees
Playing celestial symphonies;
I see the branches downward bent,
Like keys of some great instrument.

And over me unrolls on high
The splendid scenery of the sky,
Where through a sapphire sea the sun
Sails like a golden galleon,

Towards yonder cloud-land in the West,
Towards yonder Islands of the Blest,
Whose steep sierra far uplifts
Its craggy summits white with drifts.

Blow, winds! and waft through all the rooms
The snowflakes of the cherry-blooms!
Blow, winds! and bend within my reach
The fiery blossoms of the peach!

O Life and Love! O happy throng
Of thoughts, whose only speech is song!
O heart of man! canst thou not be
Blithe as the air is, and as free?

Henry Wadsworth Longfellow

Linda Nelson Stocks, an American artist living in New England, captures the carefree joy of a breezy spring day in Kites in the Wind.

Remember When

from THE KITES AND RITES OF SPRING

Marjorie Holmes

Spring is a miracle wherever it happens. Buds break, robins return, and softly, softly, stealing over the land, comes the hazing green. Like smoke unsure of its destination, it seems to hover above the trees. Then the green settles, clings, the air is golden, children beg to go wrapless to school, and everywhere is heard the perennial sounds of children in league with spring: the slap of jumping ropes, the chuckle of jacks on a flat stone step, the whirring hum of roller skates. While overhead, as if testing the sky, the kites soar.

Such things are eternal.

But who can really appreciate spring who has not spent a hard snow-shackled winter in a little town? They say the winters are changing, they don't have it so hard anymore, but when I was small in Storm Lake, Iowa, snow began to fall around Thanksgiving, and it was months before we ever saw the ground. . . . "Won't spring ever come?" you began to despair.

Then it happened, . . . The sun began to beam, the fierce white locks of winter to yield, to lose their grip. Icicles made a dripping music from the eaves, the trees stretched, shook off their white fur coats. . . .

The air was suddenly unbearably soft and sweet. You leaped the puddles or splashed recklessly through them, you ran and shouted, gone a

little mad with spring. . . .

It was time to get out your jacks or buy a little jingling bag of new ones. Time to check your skates and the size of your ball of string. Nobody had yet thought of simply sticking merchandise into a paper sack; everything you bought was wrapped in a length of paper ripped from a giant roll in the store and tied with string. And everybody saved string. An old man out near Newell was said to have achieved a roll weighing one hundred pounds. Some women of obsessive thrift and patience crocheted string into potholders and doilies, even rugs. Kids saved string for one purpose, for flying kites.

My brother, who had a paper route, could extravagantly buy his kite cord. The rest of us were content with our knotty but ever-fattening globes. Paper was saved, too. Mother would iron it for us, testing the flatiron first with a moist, sizzling finger. The paper crackled and a pleasant scorchy smell mingled with that of our flour-and-water paste. Huddled around the kitchen table, we made our kites, crossing thin pieces of wooden lathe and carefully fitting the paper around their frames. Fragile paper birds, diamond shaped, with gay tails of ribbon and colored scraps.

"Don't get it too heavy or it won't fly," we were warned.

I always knew, with a kind of sorrowing desperation, that my kite wouldn't fly anyway, no matter what. At least I couldn't make it fly. . . .

Harold could fly a kite, Gwen could fly a kite, even our little brother Barney could fly a kite, aided by our father. Mother could fly a kite, dashing along the shore with her skirts blowing back against her legs, her white teeth flashing. . . .

Farther and farther Harold would let his string out until his ship was but a speck in space. Sometimes it got away, hesitating, turning back as if to look over its shoulder for a final glimpse, struggling, not sure it wanted to leave. A wistful sense of loss and excitement would send us chasing off in the direction it was heading for a little way. Where was it going? To have fashioned something that could rise so high, travel so far before it fell—where? The bodies of runaway kites were often to be seen forlornly clutched in trees nearby—who knew where they came from? Another county maybe, another state—even from China or some other land across the sea!

FOR THE CHILDREN

Flowers

Harry Behn

We planted a garden
Of all kinds of flowers
And it grew very well
Because there were showers,
And the bees came and buzzed:
This garden is ours!

But every day
To the honeyed bowers
The butterflies come
And hover for hours
Over the daisies
And hollyhock towers.

So we let the honey
Be theirs, but the flowers
We cut to take
In the house are ours,
Not yours, if you please,
You busy bees!

You busy bees!

Playmates huddle together in a sudden shower. Photograph by Jim Whitmer Photography.

Day lilies welcome a refreshing spring shower.
Photograph by Ed Harp/Unicorn Stock Photos.

SPRING RAIN

Drops "cat-foot" on the shingles
And patter on the pane.
Sheets hammer on the tin roof;
Floods gurgle down the drain.

Trees swish in glistening garments;
Puddles drip a damp refrain.
If you have an ear for music,
You can hear it in spring rain.

O. J. Robertson

BITS & PIECES

Grant me, O God, the power to see
In every rose, eternity.
In every bud, the coming day;
In every snow, the promised May;
In every storm the legacy
Of rainbows smiling down at me!

Virginia Wuerfel

It takes both the rain and the
sunshine to make a rainbow.

Author Unknown

It ain't no use putting up
your umbrella till it rains.

Alice Caldwell Rice

Every morning the sun rises
to warm the earth. . . . The rains
come to water the earth. There is
fertility in the soil, life in the seeds,
oxygen in the air. The providence
of God is about us in unbelievable
abundance every moment.

Charles L. Allen

It is not raining rain to me,
It's raining daffodils;
In every dimpled drop I see
Wild flowers on distant hills.

Robert Loveman

The quality of mercy is not strain'd.
It droppeth as the gentle rain from heaven
Upon the place beneath.
It is twice bless'd:
It blesseth him that gives and him that takes.

William Shakespeare

Sun is delicious, rain is refreshing,
Wind braces up, snow is exhilarating.
There is no such thing as bad weather,
Only different kinds of good weather.

John Ruskin

For after all, the best thing one can do
when it's raining is to let it rain.

Henry Wadsworth Longfellow

It ain't no use to grumble
and complain,
It's just as easy to rejoice;
When God sorts out the weather
and sends rain,
Why, rain's my choice.

James Whitcomb Riley

I Am a Part

I am a part of all that I have been;
    The hawthorn's shade, the robin's wistful note,
I have the bitter berries in my heart,
    The robin's happy message in my throat.

Just as a tree is part of all the sun
    That ever shone upon its smallest leaf,
So is my heart a living manuscript
    Of all that I have known of joy or grief.

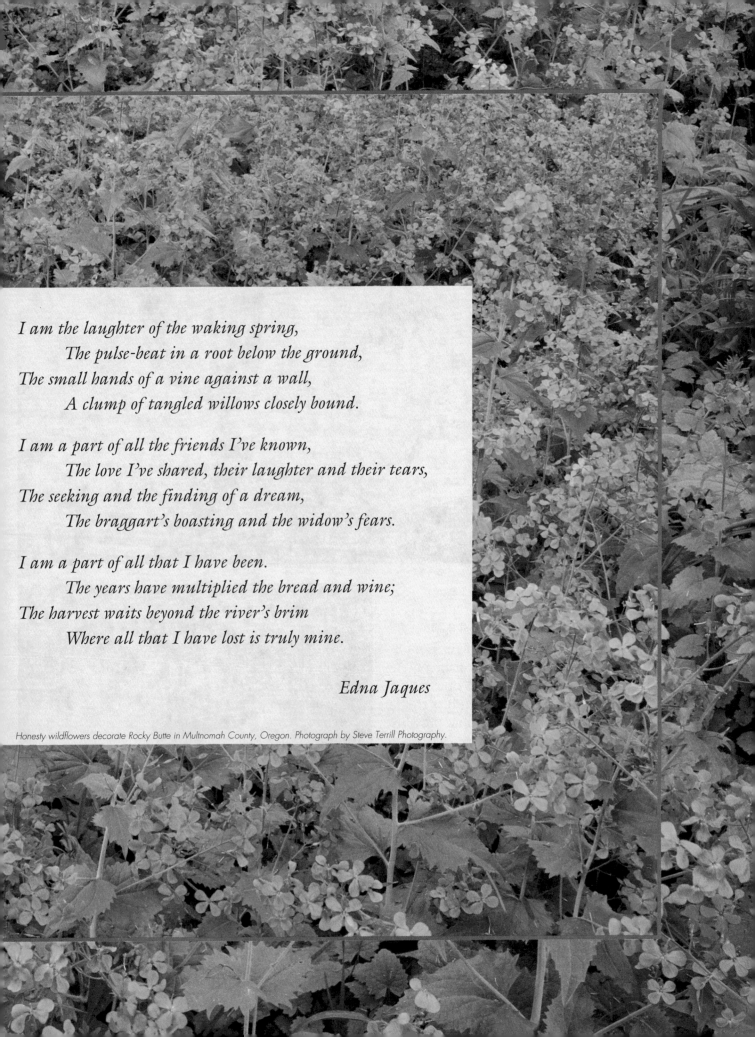

I am the laughter of the waking spring,
     The pulse-beat in a root below the ground,
The small hands of a vine against a wall,
     A clump of tangled willows closely bound.

I am a part of all the friends I've known,
     The love I've shared, their laughter and their tears,
The seeking and the finding of a dream,
     The braggart's boasting and the widow's fears.

I am a part of all that I have been.
     The years have multiplied the bread and wine;
The harvest waits beyond the river's brim
     Where all that I have lost is truly mine.

Edna Jaques

Honesty wildflowers decorate Rocky Butte in Multnomah County, Oregon. Photograph by Steve Terrill Photography.

Readers' Forum

Snapshots from Our Ideals Readers

ABOVE: Andy Straka reads an *Easter Ideals* from yesteryear to his young daughter Kelci. The Strakas live in Earlysville, Virginia, where Bonnie Foster Straka keeps busy as a physician, wife, and mother. Bonnie writes that she has her own cherished childhood memories of snuggling up with her mother to read *Ideals*. Now Bonnie and Andy share *Ideals* with Kelci and her older brother, Christopher.

RIGHT: Betty Maze shares this shot of granddaughters Kelsey and Whitney McNeil, ages two and five, with Checkers the dog. The girls love to visit Betty and her husband at their farm in Mountain City, Tennessee.

THANK YOU Andy and Bonnie Straka, Betty Maze, Sharon Hanson, and Hilda H. Morrow for sharing with *Ideals*. We hope to hear from other readers who would like to share snapshots with the *Ideals* family. Please include a self-addressed, stamped envelope if you would like the photos returned. Keep your original photographs for safekeeping and send duplicate photos along with your name, address, and telephone number to:

READERS' FORUM
IDEALS PUBLICATIONS INC.
P.O. BOX 305300
NASHVILLE, TENNESSEE
37230

ABOVE: Ean Joseph Newton of Pleasanton, California, finds out how much fun first birthdays can be. Ean is the grandson of Sharon Hanson of Mahtomedi, Minnesota, who tells us that Ean and her five other grandchildren never cease to surprise and delight her.

LEFT: Drayton Melton enjoys playing under the wild dogwood trees that dot the hillsides in Inman, South Carolina, each spring. Drayton, who is four years old, is the grandson of *Ideals* reader Hilda H. Morrow.

ideals®

Publisher, Patricia A. Pingry
Editor, Lisa C. Ragan
Copy Editor, Michelle Prater Burke
Production Manager,
   Tina Wells Davenport
Editorial Assistant, Tara E. Lynn
Contributing Editors,
Lansing Christman, Deana Deck,
Pamela Kennedy, Patrick McRae,
Nancy Skarmeas

ACKNOWLEDGMENTS

FLOWERS from *WINDY MORNING* by HARRY BEHN, copyright © 1953 Harry Behn. Copyright © renewed 1981 Alice Behn Goebel, Pamela Behn Adam, Prescott Behn and Peter Behn. Used by permission of Marian Reiner. HAPPINESS from *THE RADIANT QUEST* by Grace Noll Crowell, copyright © 1968 by Grace Noll Crowell. Reprinted by arrangement with HarperCollins Publishers, Inc. SPRING POOLS from *THE POETRY OF ROBERT FROST*, edited by Edward Connery Lathem, copyright © 1956 by Robert Frost, copyright © 1928, 1969 by Henry Holt and Company, Inc. Reprinted by permission of Henry Holt and Company, Inc. THE KITES AND RITES OF SPRING from *YOU AND I AND YESTERDAY* by Marjorie Holmes, copyright © 1973, 1987 by Marjorie Holmes. Reprinted by permission of William Morrow & Co. I BECOME A SAILOR from *UPHILL ALL THE WAY* by Edna Jaques and I AM A PART from *AUNT HATTIE'S PLACE* by Edna Jaques, copyright © in Canada by Thomas Allen and Son LImited. Reprinted by permission. ANNUAL MIRACLE from *MY HEART WAKETH* by Isla Paschal Richardson. Reprinted by permission of Branden Publishing, Boston. Our sincere thanks to the following authors whom we were unable to contact: Florence Earle Coates for FOR JOY; Alice B. Dorland for SPRING; Brian F. King for SPRINGTIME; and E. T. Scoville for MUSIC AND THE SEA.

FOXGLOVE

Spring

Spring is not so much a season
As it is a quality.

Its essence is simplicity.
Its charm lies in its freshness.
Its strength is honesty.
Its joy is ever new.

Spring is synonymous with youth.
Its inner light shines
Through the eyes of him
Who ever carries springtime in his heart.

Alice B. Dorland

UNITED STATES POSTAL SERVICE • REQUIRED BY 39 U.S.C. 3685 • STATEMENT OF OWNERSHIP, MANAGEMENT, AND CIRCULATION

1. Publication Title: Ideals. 2. Publication No.: 0019-137X. 3. Filing Date: 9/29/97. 4. Issue Frequency: 6 times a year, January, March, May, July, September, and November. 5. No. of Issues Published Annually: Six. 6. Annual Subscription Price: $19.95. 7. Complete Mailing Address of Known Office of Publication: 535 Metroplex Dr., Ste. 250, PO Box 305300, Davidson County, Nashville, TN 37230-5300. 8. Complete Mailing Address of Headquarters or General Business Office of Publisher: 535 Metroplex Dr., Ste. 250, PO Box 305300, Davidson County, Nashville, TN 37230-5300. 9. Full Names and Complete Mailing Addresses of Publisher, Editor, and Managing Editor: Publisher: Patricia A. Pingry, 535 Metroplex Dr., Ste. 250, Nashville, TN 37211; Editor: Lisa C. Ragan, 535 Metroplex Dr., Ste. 250, Nashville, TN 37211; Managing Editor: Lisa C. Ragan, 535 Metroplex Dr., Ste. 250, Nashville, TN 37211. 10. Owner (Full Name and Complete Mailing Address): Ideals Publications Incorporated, 535 Metroplex Dr., Ste. 250, Nashville, TN 37211. Stockholders Owning or Holding 1 Percent or More of Total Amount of Stock: Simon Waterlow, President, 535 Metroplex Dr., Ste. 250, Nashville, TN 37211; Martin Flanagan, Vice President, Finance, 535 Metroplex Dr., Ste. 250, Nashville, TN 37211; Patricia A. Pingry, Vice President, Publisher, 535 Metroplex Dr., Ste. 250, Nashville, TN 37211. 11. Known Bondholders, Mortgagees, and Other Security Holders Owning or Holding 1 Percent or More of Total Amount of Bonds, Mortgages, or Other Securities: Egmont Foundation, Vognmagergade II, 1148 Copenhagen K, Denmark and Trans Financial Bank, PO Box 3490, Clarksville, TN 37043. 12. For completion by nonprofit organizations authorized to mail at special rates: Not Applicable. 13. Publication Title: Ideals. 14. Issue Date for Circulation Data Below: Friendship, July 1997. 15. Extent and Nature of Circulation: Average No. Copies Each Issue During Preceding 12 Months: A. Total No. Copies (Net Press Run): 214,309. B. Paid and/or Requested Circulation: (1) Sales Through Dealers and Carriers, Street Vendors, and Counter Sales: 31,019. (2) Paid or Requested Mail Subscriptions: 162,974. C. Total Paid and/or Requested Circulation: 193,993. D. Free Distribution by Mail: 0. E. Free Distribution Outside the Mail: 0. F. Total Free Distribution: 0. G. Total Distribution: 193,993. H. Copies Not Distributed: (1) Office Use, Leftovers, Spoiled: 9,942. (2) Returns from News Agents: 10,374. I. Total: 214,309. Percent Paid and/or Requestion Circulation: 100%. Average No. Copies of Single Issue Published Nearest to Filing Date: A. Total No. Copies (Net Press Run): 159,491. Paid and/or Requested Circulation: (1) Sales Through Dealers and Carriers, Street Vendors, and Counter Sales: 4,999. (2) Paid or Requested Mail Subscriptions: 146,593. C. Total Paid and/or Requested Circulation: 151,592. D. Free Distribution by Mail: 0. E. Free Distribution Outside the Mail: 0. F. Total Free Distribution: 0. G. Total Distribution: 151,592. H. Copies Not Distribution: (1) Office Use, Leftovers, Spoiled: 7,526. (2) Returns from News Agents: 373. I. Total: 159,491. Percent Paid and/or Requested Circulation: 100%.

I certify that all information furnished is true and complete.
Rose A. Yates, Vice President, Systems and Operations